I Got Ski

Written by: Keoki Cooper-Anderson
Illustrated by: Ekeocha Nnaemeka

Keoki Cooper Anderson
Columbus, Georgia
978-0-578-36574-9

I Got Skillz

This book is dedicated to students around the world. Your mind is creative. You can create songs and even rap using the violin. Take out your violin and create a masterpiece.
You got skillz!

Another project was due in school today.
I had to think of something creative.
I wanted to report on playing basketball,
but another classmate had chosen it.

When the class went out for recess,
I didn't feel up to playing.
I sat on the swing with a basketball
thinking what else I'd be presenting.

After school I told my momma
about the project that was due
the next day.
She said I should have told her earlier
and to look around the house with haste.

I saw nada in the kitchen, nada in the den
nada in the hallway, and nada in the bin.
I slowly walked into my room
with a curious frown on my face.
I looked in the corner of my room
and saw my violin case.

"I got some skills on the violin," I thought.
I'd been playing for quite some time.
I could pluck me a melody of my own
and come up with a little rhyme.

So I sat on the front steps that day
and I began playing a little tune.
I wrote down the lyrics you see in this book.
I put my lyrics in my case in my room.

It was my turn to present my project
and I felt better that day.
With my violin in my hand and my lyrics on
my mind,
I was ready to play.

"Gotta keep ya mind moving,
show the world what ya know.
If you think ya got skillz
ya better let them skillz flow!
I got skillz!"

I Got Skillz

ACTIVITY GUIDE

Reading Comprehension

I Got Skillz is a narrative poem about a young fellow who has to decide on what to present in class. Think about what you read in this story and answer the following questions.

1. Why didn't the young fellow do his report on playing basketball?

_____

2. The young fellow used the word nada several times. What does nada mean?

_____

3. Where was the first place he looked to find something for his project?

_____

4. How was the violin useful for his project?

_____

_____

Word Unscramble

Unscramble the words below. You may look in
this book to find the answers.

1. clyri
2. niilvo
3. aadn
4. oeymdl
5. aatlklsbeb
6. ehrmy
7. cerotjp

Creating New Words

Can you create new words from a given word? Use the words below to write new words. The first one has been done for you.

1. toward- road
2. playing-
3. creative-
4. something-
5. presenting-

Rhyme With Me

Can you write a word that rhymes with each word below? Try!

The first one has been done for you.

1. When I say table you say...............able!

2. When I say mind you say............... _____

3. When I say think you say............... _____

4. When I say move you say..............._____

Word Scramble Answer Key

1. lyric
2. violin
3. nada
4. melody
5. basketball
6. rhyme
7. project

The young fellow in this book wrote this tune on a sheet of paper.

Below is the tune he played on his violin for his rap. What melody can

you create as you reread the lyrics in this book? Be creative! Enjoy!

About the Author

 Keoki Cooper- Anderson is the mother of two children.
She is a member of Alpha Kappa Alpha Sorority, Inc. Keoki has
taught general education, special education, and directed beginner
violin groups. Keoki, affectionately known as Ms. CC, has over 15
years of experience in teaching. Ms.CC recently launched her first
business known as CC's Violin Studio, LLC, which was created to
provide beginner level violin instruction. Accomplishing this goal
has always been her mission and teaching violin to children and
youth combines both her love of education and music.

Keoki aims to write books that help interested children, youth, and
even adults with understanding the uniqueness of the instrument
and the enjoyment of learning to play the Violin. Keoki plans to
continue writing poetic styled books and other inspirational books
that focus on educating others in playing the violin and moving
forward on their career paths.

Keoki resides in Georgia and holds a Specialist Degree from Walden
University in Teacher Leadership, a Master's from Walden
University, and a Bachelor's from Clark Atlanta University.

You can follow Ms.C.C. on Instagram @ keoki_cooperanderson or by visiting
www.keokicooperanderson.com